Frederick Dittmann

Let us have peace

Frederick Dittmann

Let us have peace

ISBN/EAN: 9783337224431

Printed in Europe, USA, Canada, Australia, Japan

Cover: Foto ©Thomas Meinert / pixelio.de

More available books at **www.hansebooks.com**

LET US HAVE PEACE

———o———

A MELO-DRAMA

IN THREE ACTS,

By FREDERICK DITTMANN.

———♦———

PHILADELPHIA, 1873.

DRAMATIS PERSONÆ:

COLONEL NORWOOD, a wealthy farmer, formerly Colonel of Volunteers.

WILLIAM, his Son.

JOHN, an old Sergeant.

MR. HUGHES, a Professor of Languages.

MRS. HUGHES, his Wife.

LENORA, his Daughter.

RICHARD NORTON.

MISS SOUTHWORTH, a Virginia Lady.

JAMES, her Servant. A Negro.

THE SEXTON. A SPY. A GRAVE DIGGER. SOLDIERS—

———o———

The scenes of the first and third acts are in a Village in Western Pennsylvania.

The scene of the second act in Virginia.

———o———

Time :	first	act	June,	1863.
"	second	"	Nov.	1863.
"	third	"	May,	1865.

ACT I.

WE ARE COMING FATHER ABRA'AM.

———o———

SCENE I.   A room in Col. Norwood's house·
Col. Norwood, John.
Col Norwood sitting in an arm chair at a table covered with papers.   John enters with newspapers in his hand.

JOHN.   Here, Col., are the morning papers—Great news!   At the Post Office all is excitement!   Read!   Read!

COL.   No bad news, I hope—let's see!   (*reads.*)

"Harrisburg, June 15th, 1863.

Lieutenant Palmer of the Purnell Cavalry has just come in, having fought his way from two miles this side of Green-castle.   He reports the enemy advancing in three columns, one towards Waynesburg, one towards Mercersburg, and one towards Chambersburg, other bodies are reported to be moving through the mountains making altogether six seperate columns."

And here what do I see?   A proclamation by the President of the United States, and here another from the Governor of Pennsylvania, for the turning out of the militia, and more troops.

COL.   John, I forget almost my old age and my infirmity—That it should come to this!   Our Union army defeated!   The Rebels invading our old state!   Oh!   If I were only ten—aye—five years younger!   Every good citizen—aye! moreover every soldier must feel the disgrace.

JOHN.   And I am tired reading of fighting—Whenever there was fighting to be done, I always wanted to have my hand in it, and to do my share of it; I shall go at once and enlist.

COL.   Are you, a born fool, John?   Why the wounds which you received at Wilson's Creek are not healed—and perhaps never will be.

JOHN.   Makes no difference!   The old Doctor has put so many plasters on it that, I think the skin will keep together. For an old soldier like me, it would be a shame to stay at home in such times as these.

COL.   Brave fellow!   Would to God my William had a little of your spirit.

JOHN.   That is even so, but the Devil knows—pardon, Col. the profane expression—what's got into the boy. He comes from a family whose bravery is hereditary—springs directly from old revolutionary stock—and he is—he is, what shall I say? he is so—utterly wanting in martial spirit—still I don't think he is a coward.

COL.   Where is he again?

JOHN.   Why, where he always is—squandering his time in the woods, a hunting and giving himself over to foolish dreams.

COL.   Dreams? What dreams?

JOHN.   Dreams! of course—*love* dreams—(*aside*) that was a slip of the tongue.

COL.   Love dreams?—are you crazy, John?

JOHN.   Maybe a little.

COL.   Whom should he love? There is no lady in our whole congregation—suitable to him in age—nor otherwise.

JOHN.   And if she were not of the congregation, she might be handsome nevertheless.

COL.   Nonsense, John? we are of old Puritan stock and William would never bestow his hand upon a papist. But you make me feel uneasy—do you know something? speak out!

JOHN.   I know something? God forbid! I only made the remark without—but there comes William himself.

SCENE II.   *Enters William.*

COL.   Where did you stay so long? The sun is setting, what are you doing so late in the woods and alone?

WILL.   I was standing by the brook—where I love to tarry to give myself up to meditation.

COL.   Here, my boy, I am very much dissatisfied with you.

WILL.   Certainly not more so, than I am, father, myself.

COL.   It depends upon you, whether you will satisfy us both. The cause of our country, of the Union at this present moment, looks gloomy. Look at this paper! *Pennsylvania* invaded! The capitol of the nation threatened! All the glories of our past history seem to be darkened and over shadowed with our disgrace. The eyes of the whole civilized world are fixed upon us. The enemies of republican institutions everywhere are hailing every success of the rebel army as a harbinger of the down fall of the Republic, and an overthrow of the Union. But the loyal people will not so easily abandon what is sacred to them Me thinks I hear a stentorian voice through the whole extent of this mighty land, that the Union shall and must be maintained. Everywhere people rush to arms—for the more desperate our cause becomes the more determined the American people are to uphold it. I, alas! am infirm and old—I forsooth! have to stay here and in this arm chair moan over the reverses. But look at John! He has not fully recovered from the wounds which he received at **Wilson's** Creek and now he is ready to join the first Company which goes to the front.

JOHN.   Yes, and this night.

COL.   And you! Shame upon you! My son is too big a coward to fight against the enemies of his Country and strolls about shooting rabbits.

JOHN.   Now, If *that* don't fetch him! I don't know what will.

WILL.   O, Father, how you misapprehend me! If you only knew what makes me tarry.

COL.   Silence! no excuse for an American, and one to the "manor born" like yourself, of good health and sound limbs no excuse—you hear that—when his Country calls upon him!

WILL.   (*aside*) Lenora!

JOHN.   Now, Bill, if you only had an idea how one feels when on the field of Battle! Then how the heart swells! First, when the bugle is sounded—then as you start marching to the music of the Union—then when the struggle becomes fiercer and fiercer, when the desperate attack is to be made and your Colonel is firing up your courage—you should have seen your father when he commanded us at Buena Vista. His eyes then flamed with the fires of Patriotism! Compared to them, the eyes of your sweetheart are nothing.

COL.   His sweetheart? wink just with your eyes to him—I want to know—

JOHN.   Nothing—nothing Colonel, I only meant if he had one (*aside*) Quick to something else (*aloud*) Yes, Bill, on the Battlefield a man is really a man. To loaf around at home in such times as these is humiliating. I feel certain, if you had seen our brave Lyon commanding us at Wilson's Creek, you would not stay at home another day—for just listen, how it was; Price and McCulloch out numbered us greatly and things looked gloomy—then good brave Lyon rode up before us cheered us up and that put new life into us. We carried the day--held the Battlefield---but, alas! lost our beloved General! Then it was said as with one voice:

1. We are marching to the front, boys, we are going to the fight,
   Shouting the battle cry of freedom.
   And we bear the glorius stars for the Union and the right,
   Shouting the battle cry of freedom·

      Chorus : The Union forever, Hurrah, boys. Hurrah,
              Down with the traitor, up with the star,
              For we are marching to the front boys, going to
                                          the fight.
      Shouting the battle cry of freedom.

2. We will meet the rebel host, boys, with fearless heart and true,
   Shouting the battle cry of freedom,
   And will show what Uncle Sam has for loyal men to do.
   Shouting the battle cry of freedom.

      Chorus ; The Union &c.

3. If we fall amid the fray, boys, we'll face them to the last,
   Shouting the battle cry of freedom,
   And our comrades brave shall hear us as they go rushing past.
   Shouting the battle cry of freedom.

      Chorus : The Union &c.

4. Yes, for liberty and Union we're springing to the fight,
   Shouting the battle cry of freedom,
   And the Victory shall be ours, for we're rising in our might,
   Shouting the battle cry of freedom.

      Chorus : The Union &c.

Col. Stop, old fool you! my arms are trembling and my legs won't carry me — I cannot go with you.

Will. O! that I were in the hottest of the battle!

John. (*aside to Col.*) You see now that touched him in the right place.

Will. (*aside*) If I only had not to say farewell, If I were only all at once in the field of honor when the chances would incline in favor of the enemy, and I with my men would cut our way through, save the honor of the day — the Regiment, the Army, the Country! That, then crowned with laurels, I would return to my father — ask him but

8

the one favor — he grant it, me then (*kneeling*) Father, my dear father, your blessing!

JOHN. Why now, he is running stark mad — But the old man? Won't he give it to him? —

COL. William you are a pitiful sight. But that is all the consequence of your idleness and sentimental meditations in the woods. I shall speak to your teacher

JOHN. Well, here I am —

COL. I don't mean you. Our Professor has had charge of you mostly — he shall talk to you like an old uncle —

JOHN. Beg your pardon, sir, the Professor — he his teacher? What has Bill learned from him? These old heathen languages and such stuff. I, however, have taught him what is of more use to a young American I have taught him common sense, I have shown him how to sit on horseback — how to use the sword when you are cornered — and let us get him out to the army and he will know at once what he has to do, although he stands there now like a sick old maid — he has a half of a dozen devils when he gets started once —

WILL. Yes, father, I will enlist This evening yet, I will join the company which is now being organized. And I will fight like — like — your son. But before I depart you must promise me —

COL. You will! good, good brave boy!

WILL. Will you promise that —

COL. Anything you want. Speak freely! —

                    (*knocking.*)

JOHN. (*Quick.*) Come in! aha, there is the Professor, (*aside*) He's just in time. (*to William*) For God's sake you don't know the old man. If you betray us there'll be an awful storm.

SCENE III *Enter Professor.*

PROF. How is the Colonel this evening?

COL. Thank you, very well, my dear Professor, you happen to come just at the right time. My William, your pupil, has this moment informed me that he is a going to join the Volunteers.

WILL. Yes father, so I will, if you —

PROF. (*interrupting him*) At last! God bless you! my good boy!

WILL. *(embracing him)* My dear Teacher, my father —

JOHN. Damn it! There he starts off again —

PROF. It is your duty, William. Young men, aye, even old men should hasten to respond to the call of their Country. They are coming forward from all parts of the land. And well they may — for it is to preserve the Union — and what will become of Republican institutions, were our Union to be dismembered and destroyed?

COL. Yes, Professor, but this war is for something more. The result of it must be a full verification of the Declaration of Independence — and the establishment of freedom for all, and the fullest equality before the law of all human beings who live upon American soil, and who breathe the free Atmosphere of the Western Continent. It has always troubled my conscience, my good Professor, that we so long upheld that damnable institution of slavery — and I often thought, that my bosom would be filled with remorse in my last hour — for the institution so unchristian and without the consolation of christianity what have we to give us in the dark hour ? —

JOHN. With your permission. Colonel, a good glass of Whiskey, is a good thing when one feels bad. —

COL. Shut up, you o'd fool — you are nothing but a rough soldier. —

JOHN. So I am! and —

COL. Shut up, I say.

PROF. As to that Colonel, people hold different opinions. Some think, and conscientiously too, that the Almighty has put his mark upon his creatures— that he in his infinite wisdom has so decreed that certain people are inferior to others, in intellect, in color, and in a hundred ways, But nothing of that now. The Country is in danger and we will not now inquire into the ultimate result of this war. It is enough for us to know that the Union is to be saved, and the loyal people say it shall be saved.

COL. And, as Americans we may well be proud of our people, of their patriotism, and of the alacrity with which they hasten to the rescue. However, to come to another subject Professor, you are a more learned man than I am, and you perhaps can explain to me a most singular dream. Last night, which now comes to my mind and which was thus —I stood by the side of a pond of muddy water, and saw you standing on the other side In the middle I saw a head raising itself out of the water, which resembled very much that of my William. I felt very much concerned when you, with your cane struck at it, whereupon it dived under the water and was not seen anymore.

PROF. You know what I think of dreams? that I consider them nothing more than incongruous pictures drawn by our imagination. What brought me here to day was to communicate to you — as my old neighbor, a more pleasant reality. I came to tell you, that my daughter Lenora is engaged and that this evening we are celebrating her betrothal!

WILL. A most extraordinary dream!

JOHN. That means nothing but the licking he got when he did not know his lessons.

WILL. What?

JOHN. Keep quiet! In the name of all the living devils keep quiet!

COL. I am quiet happy to hear that — and who is the happy one?

PROF. Richard Norton, generally called Dick of the Spring house.

WILL. She don't love him.

JOHN. Cannot you hold your tongue?

PROF. Never mind about that. I have to make such arrangements so as to cause her to abondon a fantastic notion which would or might make her the victim of the scheme of a certain young libertine and would plunge her into the dark abyss of female destruction.

JOHN. Well now, he goes right to the front like Genl. Lyon.

COL. Then we will both have a festival. Your daughter will be bethrothed to a stalwart young man, and my son will be married to his country — All happiness to the young handsome bride -- and — and, I shall not forget her. When are the nuptials to be?

PROF. When our Boys come back from the war and when we will celebrate the peace-festival. Then we will have the wedding.

WILL. (*aside*) Thank God! We have not peace yet,

Col.   What is the matter William ? why are you so restless ?

Prof   Will you go to the war, William ?

Will.   If my father —

Prof.   You will go. You will go with the brave boys who will leave our village to night. I have full faith in tne patriotism and bravery of my good William. You will not bring disgrace into a family with whom you have had a second home since your childhood   You will not oblige a father to curse his only daughter. May God's blessing be with you !

Will.   I cannot. What you ask of me, father, is more than human.

Prof.   Collect yourself — take courage !

John.   If I only had him out in the camp — it would soon be all right.

Prof.   And now. Col. my presence is needed at home. So I bid you all good night.

Col.   My kind regards to the happy couple and to your good old lady. (*exit Prof.*) Now, my son, get ready — and in the meanwhile I will write a few words to that excellent man, that brave soldier, my good old friend Genl. Meade ; I am satisfied he will take care of you if you are deserving of his kind disposition. John here, will be your comrade.

John.   Surely I will, and —

Will.   Father, if I am to keep my promise, you must keep yours likewise.

Col.   Of course I will, what is it ?

John.   Now we shall have an explosion —

Will.   I will march to the front — I will earn new laurels for our name and family — I will follow the flag of our Country, unto the very end of the world but — *only as the future husband of Lenora !*

Col.   Lenora !?

Will.   Only if you allow me to marry her upon my return home —

Col   Lenora !!

Will.   Lenora ! *my* Lenora !

Col.   Was that it ? Heaven, death and hell ! the bride of an. other.

WILL. Her heart knows nothing of it — She has sworn love to me.

COL. To you? you prodigal miserable boy — John call back the Professor!

JOHN. But Colonel —

COL. March!   (*John exit.*)

WILL. Father, my dear father, what are you about to do?

COL. Deprive you of every hope — make you obedient or — disown you.

WILL. Is that the love of a father for his only son?

COL. Is that the love of a son for his old father? You, my son, to marry the daughter of a papist? You so forgetful of your ancestors — our ancestors — our Puritan ancestors — and you want to bring a papist into the family? You — but enough.

WILL. And do not the papists — as you call them, worship the same God, the same Saviour?

COL. So you have these fantastic notions already? Let them pray and worship as they please — that is their business — but none of their idolatrous practices shall be introduced into my house. Just wait one moment and I will show you how I will handle your future father-in-law who made such good use of the time which I thought you spent in his house in pursuing your studies — Why, I am convinced he has schemed this marriage — It is all a preconcerted affair.

WILL. Upon my honor, father, he —

COL. Silence! Don't waste your honor, you — you — who wants to disgrace our family.

WILL. With all respect for our ancestors, father — I solemnly believe that the day is happily gone by in this free land of ours, when any destinction is made on account of creed or nationality. Catholics signed the Declaration of Independence — Catholics fought in the revolutionary war, were your comrades in Mexico — Catholics are distributing charity everywhere to day as well as Protestants or Hebrews — and we all understand by this time that the creed is something — I don't know what to call it — and a that it is true, honest, brave and charitable heart, which makes the good man. And I, sir, I swear to you now, that I love her, that I shall never

abandon her, that she shall be .nine — that I shall take
her home to my bosom, even if we were to celebrate our
nuptials in the dismal swamp of Virginia or in the wild
forests of the far west.

COL. Celebrate them where you please — dance it out on the
grave yard — where your murdered father will lie buried — if that does suit you !

WILL. O God! Why should man have these agonies? Are not
thy heavens grand in their azure blue? Are not thy
meadows dresse din green — are not thy forests free —
and why should we — we men, be slaves to our old prejudices?

SCENE IV. *Enter Prof. and John.*

PROF, You surprise me Colonel.

COL. You may well be surprised, old hypocrite.

PROF. Colonel !

COL. You dared to entice — over in your rookery — to draw
my boy into love affairs. May the devil hold the candle
for that job to you and your women folks.

PROF. Colonel — I beseech you to keep within the bounds of
moderation. ---

COL. Within the bounds of moderation ?! You undertake to
say that to me and in my own house ? Who are you sir?
Have you forgotten that you came to this place years
ago, poor, penniless, wretched ? Did I not protect you ?
Did I not --- to help you --- engage you a tutor to my
boy — and did I not obtain for you, other pupils ---
enabling you to earn a livelihood ? And now are those
my thanks, that you --- not only entice my son
away from his father --- but, command me to keep within the bounds of moderation ! ---

PROF. (*solemnly*) I know, sir, that I am a poor man and I am
not ashamed to acknowledge it --- I never had riches and
never squandered a fortune. But sir. I am an honest
man, and I am proud to say it. You, sir. may be proud
of your revolutionary ancestors --- nobody is respon-
sible for the stock from which he springs. That is the
dispensation of Providence. You, may be proud of
your military achievements, I sir, have done my duty
in my sphere --- in educating the young so that they
might become good citizens. And while employed in

that occupation, I have done perhaps as much good for the country as you or any one, who has led the life of a soldier. You, tell me, that you assisted me when I was a stranger in this place — with nothing but my education and my knowledge — And as to that, I will say to you that I always felt as if under the burden of a heavy debt to you for that act of kindness — but you sir, have relieved me. I stand on a level with you now; for he who throws up to any one an act of kindness has no future claim to gratitude or recognition. I am opposed to a union of my daughter with your son, because I know what religious prejudices will do — and you have given me the best illustration of it this evening, Now, sir, I which you a good evening — and I would also have you to remember, that I expect to be treated respectfully as a respectable man has a right to. (*exit.*

JOHN. Well now, Colonel, the Professor talks right plain and comes straight to the front like Genl. Lyon.

COL. He was — he was right. I feel ashamed of myself.

WILL. He spoke to the point — and so will I. If I may not marry Lenora I'll put a bullet through my brain!

COL. You will ? — JOHN (*whispering something in his ear.*)

JOHN. (*hesitatingly*) Colonel — but —

COL. March !

JOHN. A hell of a day this evening! (*exit*)

WILL. Have you no answer for me ? —

COL. Patience, my boy, patience ! —

(*pause*)

Enters John with two pistols, which he puts upon the table.

COL. Here is my answer. Here the one for you the other for me.

WILL. Father !

COL. Take them! They are loaded or perhaps you have not the courage to blow your brains out. Then direct the weapon upon me ! Do your best now — and when I am dead bestow your hand upon this papist girl — Go on !

WILL. (*kneeling*) Father, have mercy ! —

COL. One word more — Either you go up to your room — pack up what things you want to take along and join the Company which is to start from here to night — or

--- you may go where you please --- for I want nothing of you. No more --- not a word! John come with me --- after a little while I shall be back and see if I have a son or not.

JOHN, Colonel --- the pistols!

COL. Leave them here. The Almighty gave him his life --- if he wants to commit waste, I shall not deprive him of the privilege! Better dead than dishonored. Come John (*Exeunt Col. and John.*)

WILL. Yes, yes! I must go --- must leave this place, must leave her, must find her when I return as his wife! by heavens! must I?! No! No! --- Father left the pistols here --- he said I could do with my life what I pleased. So will I, shall I live without her? No, no --- (*taking a pistol*) So small a thing can put an end to so much misery --- Aye, my comforter (*cocking the pistol*) that is the first pull --- one pull more and it is done --- (*a long pause*) But the consequences --- what will Lenora say --- it will drive her to despair, perhaps to madness --- my father--- I shudder to think of it --- (*lays down the pistol*) (*pause*) What Lenora, the wife of that fellow, what interest to me what becomes of her? Father, himself has put the pistol here for me — he has no heart, he does not feel for me --- (*taking the pistol*) What do I care for all of them when I am dead and gone, when I have left a world which has nothing attractive for me. The Almighty has not fixed his cannon against self slaughter. He, in his infinite mercy will forgive me if I quit a life which is nothing but a burden to me. One pull and all is over --- and this poor soul may have rest --- So good bye world, good bye Father, good bye Lenora --- (*raising the pistol --- a drum and fife are heard outside*). My friends the companions of my boyhood are a gathering to march to the front. They have courage to face the cannon of the enemy (*pause*) (*throwing the pistol on the table.*) away tempter! I will live --- I have courage to face the enemy --- If I find my death on the battlefield it will be an honorable death --- I will live --- I am no coward --- I will show it. I will be a man from this day (*pause.*) a Suicide is --- at best --- a miserable coward --- a runaway --- who because he fears the adversities of life --- wants to escape them by self destruction. I will live and I will live for my Country! (*exit.*)

Scene V. John (*with knapsack and a soldiers mantel.*)

No I cannot stand it any longer here! Out in the camp on the field — there is my place! There they fight with the bayonet and with the sword! There I feel at home — Here where they fight battles of words is not my place — Come old mantle. Give me protection once more against rain, and snow, and storm. Here the moths will eat thee, better we be used up and worn out in our proper sphere — Only last me until I have to depart to join the grand army of yonder world.

(*Sings.*)   I wear thee now these eighteen years :
We've passed through storms severe —
When the cannon balls were flying,
And the boys around us dying
We too did never fear.

And often in the stilly night,
When rain and snows did fall,
Thou! thou alone did'st warm me,
And whatsoever did harm me,
Old mantle, thou know'st it all!

And tales thou never told'st on me :
Wast faithful thou wast true —
Wast true 'gainst all contending,
Of thee there shall be no mending —
Lest mantle, thou should'st become new —

And may they laugh and mock at me.
Thou art precious to my soul
For where the tatters are hanging suspended.
Their way the bullets wended
Each bullet makes a hole.

And when the bullet comes at last
That pierces through the heart,
Then, while my eyes are breaking
My comrades shall be speaking
Thus should a soldier depart.

When taken to the dark cold grave
My friends, I want no crowd ;
Six soldiers my corpse shall carry
And on their way not tarry
This mantle be my shroud.

SCENE VI. JOHN. *Enter several Volunteers.* .

1. VOL. Where is the Colonel? where is William? -.-
JOHN. Why?
2. VOL. We were appointed a Committee to inform William
that we have unanimously chosen him our Captain, and
before leaving desire to pay our compliments to the
Colonel.
JOHN. That shows good sense in you --- You have made an excellent choice. ---
3. VOL. And it is the wish of the Company that you should be
our first Lieutenant.
JOHN. I! no --- Thank you for the honor, but your SERGEANT
I will be. I want my rifle as well as my sword when I
go into battle
(*Enter William*) Here is a Committee to inform you
that the Company haselected you their Captain --- You,
of course, will accept.
WILL. I will --- at the head of the Company I will fight and die
--- where the bullets are showering there shall be my
place - - are you soon ready to start.
A VOL. Yes sir --- when will you meet us to take the command?
JOHN. Leave that to me. I will make the arrangements. (*Ex-
eunt Volunteers*)
WILL. One favor do me yet, John --- Go over to the Professor
and tell Lenora --- (*pause crying*)
JOHN. (*aside*) Rather would I fight the battle of Wilson's Creek
over again than see the poor boy thus (*aloud*) you might
go yourself, Bill
WILL. Do you think so?
JOHN. So much time you will have to spare to say farewell to
her, perhaps it is forever.
WILL. Forever? do you count all Eternity for nothing?
JOHN. Soldiers and Eternity have nothing to do with each
other. (*Exeunt*)
SCENE VII. *An open space at the gate of the Prof's. garden.*
LENORA, RICHARD NORTON.

RICH. I feel embarassed.
LENO. I see that.
RICH. Therefore you might meet me half ways --

Leno. How?

Rich. With friendship.

Leno. I always felt friendly towards you. ---

Rich. With love. ---

Leno. I — I I have to much respect for you ---

Rich. Upon respect and confidence true love is based.

Leno. Mr Norton --- I --- I (*aside*) No I cannot tell him.

Rich. You make me sad. Miss Lenora ---

Leno. There is Miss Wilson, your neighbour's daughter ---

Rich. That conceited old maid!

Leno. She is far more handsome than I am --- and it is said she had an eye on you ---

Rich. I see none but Lenora's eyes ---

Leno. (*aside*) He wont understand me ---

Rich. You seemed to favor me. ---

Leno. But I cannot --- I cannot *love* you! Aye my dear Mr. Norton, my father is so severe with me. --- Be my protector.

Rich. (*walking up to her*) That is just what I desire to be ---

Leno. (*Retreating*) Not in this way, from a distance.

Rich. Why?

Leno. Because - - because --- I --- I love another man --- (*aside*) Thank God! it is out.

Rich. That is only a youthful notion. A kind husband, and I promise to be such, will soon make you forget him.

Leno. Is he not to be shaken? ---

Rich. There comes your father.

Leno. If you mean to be a friend to me, don't betray me ---

Scene VIII. *Enter the Professor.*

Prof. Do I find you together and alone? --- That is right, that is what I like to see. Always be so. Come into the house --- exchange rings and receive my blessing ---

Rich. Friend, teacher --- father! ---

Leno. (*with a tremulous voice*) father! ---

Prof. Silence! Your obedience, and it only can make me forget, what I suffered on your account. Call your mother!

Rich. She is crying! --- I will dry her tears, Aye! Lenora I will carry you on my hands! ---

PROF. Did I live to suffer that? Did I survive the insult? When, O when will the time come, when men will recognize each other as brethren.

SCENE IX. *Enter Mrs. Hughes.*

PROF. Lenora is a bride.

MRS. H. So I hear. ---

PROF. We will celebrate the bethrotal this day. - -

MRS. H. You think so?

PROF. William goes to the army to night. I will not know what share you had in my disgrace ---

MRS. H. Disgrace?

PROF. What it should come to that! Happy as we were in our honest poverty --- and this thunderstorm should come over us! But I forgive you.

MRS. H. Dear Husband!

PROF. Be quiet --- Don't speak any more about it. *(Exeunt through the gate).*

SCENE X. *Enter John and William.*

JOHN. Now you see how you get her to come out --- I will go and make the arrangements; when the boys start to march to the depot---I shall come to call you *(exit John.)*

WILL. The old signal is the best. But I am trembling, my heart is panting. Dear home, I approach thee for the last time. Dear old hammer for the last time thou knockest at this gate.

        (a bugle sound is heard at a distance)

That is the sound now they call me --. Lenora come into my arms *(knocks three times on the gate)* *(Lenora comes rushing out.)*

LENO. O! William, do you come to my betrothal?

WILL. To bid you farewell!

LENO. You go —

WILL. To the war —

LENO. And I remain here —

WILL. In the arms of a lover.

LENO. I hate him — I only love you —

WILL. Will you be true to me —

LENO. As true as I live —

Will.   Swear !

Leno.   By the living God ! by my honor — by the life of my parents ! But no ! what is everything to me, compared to you ? I swear to be true to you by the love with which I love you.   And you ?

Will.   Yours forever and ever.   Your father said when the company returns from the war, your nuptials are to be. Before they all come back, I will be here — and if your parents will not cave in, we will elope.

Leno.   I shall follow you — and if necessary to the grave.

Will.   The night before your wedding you will hear me knock at the gate.

Leno.   I shall fly up, count one, two, three.   You will be there — I rush into your arms !

Will.   You throw yourself on my bosom — over yonder at the graveyard gate I shall have my horse standing — I carry you over there — we mount the horse, and then —

Leno.   But William if you should not return. f you should fal in battle — if —

Will.   *I shall come anyhow!*

Leno.   Do not blaspheme the Almighty ! —

Will.   Who says that I do ? my love is so great that it reac he far beyond the grave. I shall come, I call you --- I shal not leave you Lenora — and if I had to tear you from the Altar when the minister is to solemnize the marriage — aye! if I had to drag you out from the bridal chamber —

Leno.   Take this ring.   My intended one has forced it upon my finger.   Give me your ring — so, now it is all wel we are betrothed —

Will.   For this and for yonder world ! O Lenora — I hold you in my arms — let us elope — away to the West — found an humble home — and live contended and happy, for where there is love there is happiness.

Leno.   William ?! my father — no matter how he stands in our way — he is my father still —

Will.   Come, come ! I won't let you go ! —

Mrs. H (*from within*) Lenora !

Leno.   Woe ! my mother !

Will.   Your mother is not against us !

Leno.   But she cannot do anything with father.

MRS. H. (*as before*) Your father asks for you — why do you tarry, Lenora !

LENO. I am coming —

SCENE XI. *Enter John.*

JOHN. William — it is time ---

(music is heard behind the scenes.)

LENO. Farewell, William ! ---

WILL. (*embracing her*) Lenora !

LENO. Be true !

WILL. Unto death !

MRS. H. Lenora !

LENO. In a minute, mother --- be true ? ---

WILL. Unto death aye ! beyond the grave !

JOHN. Come, come away!

(*Exeunt Lenora through the garden gate. Enter the Company, William and John marching in military order, then Colonel Norwood dressed in Continental uniform.*)

COL. You drop the plow to follow the flag of your Country, You throw aside the hoe to seize the sword --- You do right boys! That is what our forefathers did --- This uniform my grandfather wore at Bunker Hill. May the same spirit which animated them prevail with you --- and when you return and the Union is saved --- and I should be dead by that time --- Come to my grave and let me know the glorious news --- Sing out to me but these Words: the Union is saved --and I shall hear them --- though I were under the ground a mile deep !

And now William, the boys have chosen you their Captain --- do honor to the position --- Here I present you with the very sword which my grandfather wielded at Bunker Hill, the same my father carried when fighting under the great and good Jackson at New Orleans and the same which was mine at the battle of Buena Vsta. --- Do Justice to it (*pause*)

JOHN. Colonel! you --- pardon me --- better don't undertake to make a speech --- you never were much of a talker --- Our Captain takes right after you, and that is all right -- Great Captains were always noted for their silence --- Now if you allow me I will tell the Boys all you want to say --- and I will tell them in my own plain way ---

MUSIC.

(*Song.*) We are coming, Father Abraham.
Three hundred thousand more :
From Mississippi's winding stream.
And from New England shore.
We leave our plows and workshops,
Our wives and children dear ;
With hearts too full of utterance
With but a silent tear.
We dare not look behind us.
But steadfastly before.
We are coming. Father Abraham.
Three hundred thousand more !

Chorus. We are coming, We are coming.
Our Union to restore :
We are coming, Father Abraham,
With three hundred thousand more.

If you look across the hill tops.
That meet the Northern sky.
Long moving lines of rising dust.
Your vision may descry,
And now the wind an instant,
Tears the cloudy veil aside,
And floats aloft our spangled flag.
In glory and in pride.
And bayonets in the sunlight gleam.
And bands brave music pour —
We are coming. Father Abraham.
Three hundred thousand more !

Chorus. We are coming. &c.

If you look all up our valleys.
Where the growing harvest shine,
You may see our sturdy farmer boys.
Fast forming into line,
And children from their mothers knees.
Are pulling at the weeds.
And learning how to reap and sow,
Against their country's needs.
And a farewell group stands weeping
At every cottage door —
We are coming. Father Abraham.
Three hundred thousand more !

Chorus. We are coming. &c.

You have called us, and we're coming,
By Richmond's bloody tide ;
To lay us down for freedom's sake,
Our brothers' bones beside ;
Or from foul treason's savage group
To wrench the murderous blade :
And in the face of foreign foes,
Its fragments to parade.
Six hundred thousand loyal men,
And true have gone before —
We are coming. Father Abraham.
Three hundred thousand more !

Chorus.   We are coming, &c.

(*Marching and countermarching on the stage,
during which the curtain drops.*)

END OF ACT I.

————o.————

ACT II.

A GOOD MENTOR.

Scene I.   Garden surrrounded by a high wall on the side of it
an arbor

Miss Southworth, James, and John.

Miss S. That is all well and good, but enough of that now ---
Be pleased to leave us.

John.   I'll go Miss ---

Miss S.   What is it you want ?

John.   Nothing --- You won't get him though, as long as I live
--- (*exit*)

Miss S.   Impudent fellow! (*after looking around*) How now ?
No news ?

James.   From Col. Saunders ? No, not yet.   O Miss, how pas-
sionately he loves you, over in yonder wood, he keeps
himself, now looking over here and sighing for you, and
you here --- wishing that you were with him.

MISS S. Stop your balderdash! Since when are you my confident that you speak so familiarly to me. Understanme, sir, no more such talk! Be gone, sir, I see the Mdjor coming.

JAMES. I always fear —

MISS. S· What?

JAMES. You might let that Yankee take too good and deep a peep into your cards.

MISS S. (*Wants to answer but restrain's herself and beckons to him to go— he does so shaking his head)* I play a dangerous game! To the Colonel I feel attached by a common purpose — by politics and by a common hatred of these Yankee invaders — William — I love — without him I cannot live — Could I but gain him over to our Cause — but he does not understand me — or perhaps don't want to — and that were far better (*meditating*).

SCENE II. WILLIAM (*looking at her*) There she is!

WILL. Here beautiful, Miss?

MISS S. You here Major? whence did you come?

WILL. Came directly from Headquarters —

MISS S. Anything new there?

WILL. All are in good cheer and hopeful —

MISS S. Because they think our cause a lost one —

WILL. Even so — why should we not think so? Since we deafeated your army at Gettysburg — Since —

MISS. S· I am sorry to tell you, that you are laboring under a most deceitful declusion — Our Southern people can never be conquered — we are invincible — By this time you might have satisfied yourselves of their bravery — and not only that — you know the French are in Mexico looking over thborder?

WILL. I know what you mean to say, and let me answer you --- that you are only deceiving yourself. That the Southern people --- are brave is true --- and I am proud of them on that account for I cannot forget that they are Americans --- but as to the French --- never mind them! ---

MISS. S. And are you not of the opinion they sympathize with us, in our struggle?

Will. Certainly 1 am --- but what good will it do you?

Miss S. What harm will it do you?

Will. None whatever, one of these days -- Old Mr. Seward will send a little notice to Napoleon - - telling him that Uncle Sam does not relish the sight of foreign mercenaries trespassing so near his own ground

Miss S. And Napoleon?

Will. Will send his ships to take his soldiers home ---

Miss S. Do not deceive yourself. That is just the stuff your Government is circulating among the people --- The aims of the French Emperor are higher -- he does not want to see a free and gallant people oppressed. We shall have assistance before long if we need it.

Will. Miss, don't proceed any further --- I cannot comprehend how an American lady could wish a foreigner to come, and glory in the humiliation of our Common Country.

Miss S. Our Common Country?! we have no Common Country We have on one side --- on our side a free people struggling for Independence, and on your side --- the Invaders --- coming to subjugate --- to enslave us people of the South --- Abstain, Major, from your purpose; the Union is severed ---

Will. Never! Never! as long as the stars and stripes are waving, the cause of the Union is not hopeless.

Miss S. That cause is lost! is irredeemably lost --- and all who adhere to it -- are lost with it.

Will. Then let it be so! Better go down with the flag of our country waving, than live to triumph upon her ruins ---

Miss. S (animated) May our enemies be destroyed---All! all! Only one I should want to save --- only one ---for to gain him over to our side!

Will. I dare not understand these words --- else --- I should have to treat one --- whom I worship --- as a public enemy.

Miss S. Worship?

Will. Let us drop the subject. The future will develope all.

Miss S. What the future will bring us --- We can easily foresee. Your stubbornness makes you ignore a friend, who would be willing to stake her fate with yours --- but (imitating him) let us drop the subject.

WILL. You mock me. ---

MISS S. Go to! let me alone! Go among your rough Yankee soldiers! Listen to that old ruffian of a Sergeant. What do you care if you should break my heart. Perhaps in bloody combat you may meet one of my brothers --- and what a triumph for a young hero ---

WILL. Miss! Dear Miss! Do you want to kill me? you are torturing me to death. Since I know you, I have lost my cheerfulness --- the peace of my heart is disturbed --- must you torment me thus? You know, dear Miss, that I am engaged at home ---

MISS. S. Must I hear that?

WILL. Engaged to one who is true to me -- who loves me --- who ---

MISS. S. Is that it?

WILL. But I have already been faithless to her! New aspirations are occupying my mind. Your graciousness has made me bold--- Miss, have I been deceived?

MISS. S. (Jestingly) Traitor!

WILL. Woe to me! a Traitor!

MISS S. Never mind --- I was not serious. ---

WILL. (aside) Yes, a traitor ---a traitor to her, a Traitor to my Country! You are an enemy of our country ---

MISS S. I only said so in a Jest---Have confidence in me---I will be your guide;

WILL. (taking her hand) How that touch electrifies me, I am lost (kneeling)

MISS S. My dear young enthusiastic warrior! There are laurels in store for this brow! Could I but crown it---Bethink yourself --- take sides for southern independence!

WILL. Cruel girl! How you let me feel that I wear shackles --- and that I am your slave ---

MISS S. But those shackels are of flowers ---

WILL. Under which treason is lurking. But my dear miss --- my manhood is yours --- I am completely in your power --- O Miss --- could I be yours?

MISS S. Be ours --- and you are mine! ---

WILL. Where am I --- I am losing my senses ---
                        (leaning his head on her arm)
MISS S. (aside) He is caught.

(Enter James.)

JAMES. Your presence is requested —
MISS S. Excuse me for a moment.

Exeunt Miss S. and James.

WILL. What a change that woman has worked in me. I am
almost a stranger to myself! Here in the sunny south
everything attracts me — The south is the paradise —
and Miss Southworth is put a watch at the gate — beckons to me to come over, but a sense of duty keeps me
back. How fine it must be — How blessed the land on
the Mississippi — on the Gulf - And when the war is
over, I have to go back to the sterile soil in the mountains of Pennsylvania — I —

Enter John. (tapping him on the shoulder.

JOHN. Major !
WILL. What do you want here ?
JOHN. What is the matter, Major ?
WILL. What is that to you ?
JOHN. Well now, I suppose I might ask the question. I saw
this Miss Southworth just leave you, and I thought I
would speak to you a word or two. Major, you ought
to be ashamed of yourself!
WILL. You dare sir ?
JOHN. I dared nothing yet — the best is to come —
WILL. Silence! Let me alone !
JOHN. Yes, I believe it, you would like to shake me off, for
when the conscience is not in the right trim we cannot
very well look honest people in the face. But sir, I
won't go — at least not without you — You have advan-
ced too far, and it becomes necessary to sound a re-
treat. I suppose you understand me ?
WILL. Does that intruder dare to remind me of my duty ?
(aloud) Shall I teach you what subordination means?
Attention: About face ! not a word or by the Eternal—
JOHN. *(puts himself in a military posture.) (pause)*
WILL. John ! —
JOHN. Hem ! —
WILL. John ! —
JOHN. Well ? —
WILL Speak ? —

(pause.)

JOHN. When twenty four years ago, you first saw light, I had not a grain of respect for you. Now however you have grown above me — and are my Major — and of course, I have to obey orders — But I am not blind for all that and I see but too well that this handsome secesh girl has put the sling right around your neck. If your father would know that? Now, in the first place, you commit a sin against your father — for he is a staunch old Union man. We have now the year '63, now you were born — let see — take 24 from 63 — 4 from 3 won't go — therefore I borrow one - - 4 from 13 leaves 9, and 2 from 5 leaves 3 --- 39 --- If I had known then that you would thus disgrace us? But you may abuse me, for you are my Major --- you may knock and kick me about --- that is nothing, that is the lot of true old servants and of old dogs ---

WILL. John!

JOHN. O, that is all nothing! You gave the command Attention! About face! And here I stand like a bronze statue. You also commanded me to speak --- Now secondly you commit a great sin against Lenora ---

WILL. Who mentioned that name?

JOHN I did! Old Sergeant John. ---

WILL. John, forgive me! *(putting his arms around his neck)*

JOHN. I stand firmly, and am a fort you cannot take so easily. But, Major, let go --- if the boys should see it --- that don't look well, for a Major.

WILL. On this breast my head rested when I was a mere infant, with these whiskers the boy played! Forgive me John!

JOHN. Major --- will you allow me to raise my right hand for a moment --- a few drops of water just rolled down my cheeks and they tickle so in my whiskers --- just let me wipe them off — I feel as if every drop of blood that is in me — were stirred up.

WILL. You awake me from my dream — John what shall I do?

JOHN. Be true to Lenora — sack this girl — The she devil is cunning.

WILL. Miss Southworth loves me —

JOHN. Possibly. — Lenora surely. —

WILL. Miss Southworth is sincere with me. —

JOHN. Don't you believe it — she is false.

WILL. For the first time in this fearful ordeal my first love recurs to my mind. I see Lenora's window, I hear her sweet voice! I also see our parents —

JOHN. They were always in your way — why did you not care for them formerly? This won't do. You have given your promise to Lenora — and a man that would break such a promise, is no man at all — and is not worthy to live among decent people — Yes, William you are in the fair way to be false to your sweet heart, and then turn traitor to your Country. —

WILL. John — do you want to kill me?

JOHN. Not at all — I want to bring you back to a right and honorable life! Is it not a shame — Here we are gone five months, and you have written to her but once! What must her mother think of you; And she was always on your side — you know?

WILL. But what shall I write?

JOHN Why, you don't know that? Here, sit down by this table — take out your book. tear out a leaf, and I will tell you —

> (Sings.) 1. When thinking how I wronged thee
> My heart feels sad and sore,
> I am sad beyond all measure
> I shall wrong thee never more —
>
>   2. I know for me thy prayers,
> Were said by night and day,
> Thou had'st no happy hour
> Since I have been away.

I give that to you in my own plain style. You must put it in the right shape yourself and give it the proper polish. The sense of it — I guess is about correct for true love is always the same — It was always alike fifty years ago and now — with majors and sergeants — And the infidelity of a lover always looks black — therefore you must write:

(Sings.) 3. I never shall forsake thee —
And should it be my lot
To die in gory battle,
I shall forget thee not.

4. Thou art my precious treasure —
Thou art forever mine,
And whether I am living
Or dead, still I am thine,

(William writing.)

JOHN. Will that letter be long yet?

WILL. Why ?

JOHN. When you come to turn over I should like to say something. But just write ahead! I hope I don't disturb you by talking a little. Now, Major --- when we have defeated these gray Jackets and are coming home, and everything is straightened up, then I shall speak to the Colonel, your father, I should say, and then I shall tell him that his William, came near turning traitor to his Country --- that he was led astray by the Charms of a Virginia lady, and that it was his love for Lenora which saved him --- Now if the old man don't cave in when he hears that --- well then I don't know him.

WILL. Lenora! Lenora ! How could I thus forget thee ?

JOHN. Yes it was high time --- but now I want the letter mailed forthwith   The anguish of the poor girl about you must be great indeed. *(Exeunt)*

SCENE III. *A camp scene. Tents in the back ground.*

1st V. Alas! this picket duty --- it is awful --- a body may almost die, because he don't know how to spend his time ---

2nd V. Nonsense --- we knew that before we enlisted that a campaign has its hardships. Did you not notice any suspicious signs?

1st V. No -- what should it have been ?

2nd V. Why, I was stationed near that bridge over yonder --- and I saw men a moving to and fro, who did not appear to be regular confederate soldiers, they looked to me very strange.

1st V. Go to! When you have been on duty you always want to make out that you were especially vigilant.

2nd V. And when you are at a picket post --- you never think that it is vigilance, and vigilance above all you should exercise ---

1st V. I know my duty just as well as you know yours ---

2nd V. From your conversation it don't seem so ---

1st V. I won't be insulted.

2nd. V. And I won't take any of your lip ---

Other Volunteers come to the front.

3rd V. What are you quarreling about?

1st and 2nd V.
I don't want to be insulted ---

3rd V. Look here boys --- they are quarreling --- we won't have it --- Better Dutchie give us a song, that will put things to right·

Sevl. V. Yes, yes --- Dutchie give us that dutch song of yours.

(Dutchie sings.)

If you're going, says he,
To yonder land, says he,
Take your Sallie, says he,
By the hand, says he,
You cannot enter, says he,
Through the throng, says he,
If your Sallie, says he,
Isn't along.

Would'nt go, says he,
Would'nt stir says he,
At the gate, says he,
Without her, says he,
Without my darling, says he,
I would'nt be glad, says he,
Without Sallie, says he,
I should be sad.

And her hand, says he,
Is so neat, says he,
And her kiss, says he,
Is so sweet, says he,
And her arm, says he,
Is so round, says he,
Let a sick man kiss it,
And he feels sound.

And her hair, says he,
Is like flax, says he,
And her heart, says he,
Soft as wax, says he,
She has a bosom, says be,
White as snow, says he,
She has feet, says he,
Like a roe.

(*Enter William and John.*)

JOHN. What is all this? are you cutting your capers again? Is this a time for such nonsense? Are you soldiers! You ought to remember that your blue blouse covers a citizen and that you should be thinking fighters, and not mere war machines, like the soldiers of an Europeon King There they may cajole — for there they have nothing to think of, but how to depose one King, and to make an Emperor of the other. There they may sing and dance, but here you ought never to forget that War is a serious thing —

WILL. (*aside to John*) Don't be over particular with the boys!

JOHN. (*To Will*) I don't mean it so hard, but we must always have an eye to discipline.

(*A voice is heard behind the scenes*) Come this way!

(*Enter several soldiers, with a ragged young negro.*)

A SOLD. Major, we caught this nigger, and he will not give a full account of himself, saying that he must see an officer.

NEGRO. Captain!

JOHN. (*aside to negro*) Say Major; he is our major!

NEGRO Major! Don't hurt me — the soldiers there thought I was a spy — but I am not — I run away from my Massa Col. Saunders — and got through the lines — over there near that bridge, they fired several shots at me — but only one bullet hit me, here in my left hand — but I didn't mind that. Major, I have som thing to tell you (*looking at the soldiers.*)

(*John beckons to the soldiers.*) (*they retire to the back of the stage.*)

NEGRO. My master, and a good many others, have arranged matters to take the President a prisoner and hurry him off to the South, and want to capture him when he takes his drive to the Soldiers Home, a number of men are engaged for the Job. And I believe are stationed in the woods, and they are the ones who shot at me. From what I could understand, they have parties to assist them in Maryland and have made all preparations to cross the Potomac below Acquia creek during the night, and then with all speed go to Washington. After the President has been taken away, the Confederates can surprise the Union Army, and take the capitol. There is a lady living some where in this neighborhood who is also connected with the plot. My master wants to marry her.

JOHN. Did you hear the name of that woman?

NEGRO. Yes I heard her called Miss Southworth.

(*John casts a triumphant look at William who nods.*)

Oh, Major make all haste to save the President for they are all ready and may go about the business any minute. For God's sake, Major, I am no spy, and believe me. You may perhaps think, that it is not worth your while to listen to me, that I am but a poor nigger, but all I have told you is true. Don't send me back to my Master.

WILL. Good, good poor fellow! I believe you, and I shall not send you back to your Master, but here give me your hand; you are a free man from this day. I shall defend your liberty, even at the cost of my own life. Oh how wonderful are the ways of Providence, you owe your country the least, love her the most. Where others had liberty and all enjoyments of life, you have been wearing your shackels, and the reward of your labor, was probably poor food and the lash. Verily! If there be an All, Just and Merciful God in Heaven, and a logic in history, this war can never come to an end, until your rights are fully established and secured.

JOHN. Well now Major, that's all very good, I have felt that same way all along, although I know nothing of what you call logic of history, but men of my sort never studied such learned stuff. We have to travel through life somewhat like a blind man, we have to feel our way as we go along.

And what is the difference so we arrive at the same spot with you. There is for instance that good old philosopher in New York, his reasoning faculty always seems to me to be located in the heart, and he takes the right view of things for all that. Now if you will listen to me a moment, I will tell you how I feel on the subject and the boys may hear it too!

(*He turns toward the soldiers.*

Come forth boys, I have something to tell you?

(*Soldiers coming to the front of the stage, and gather around William and John.*)

If what I have to say, should be to your liking, you may put an oar in, too.

First however, let the band strike up; music always loosens my tongue.

John Brown's body lies mouldering in the grave,
John Brown's body lies slumbering in the grave,
But John Brown's soul is marching with the brave,
His soul is marching on.

Chorus.   Glory, Glory Hallelujah!
Glory, Glory Hallelujah!
Glory, Glory Hallelujah!
His soul is marching on.

He has gone to be a soldier in the army of the Lord,
He is sworn as a private in the ranks of the Lord,
He shall stand Armageddon with his brave old sword,
When Heaven is marching on.

Chorus.   Glory, &c,

He shall file in front when the lines of battle form,
He shall face to front when the squares of battle form,
Time with the column and charge with the storm,
When men are marching on.

Chorus.   Glory, &c.

Ah! foul tyrants do you hear him as he comes?
Ah! foul traitors do you know him as he comes,
In the thunder of the cannon and the roll of the drums,
As we go marching on?

Chorus.   Glory, &c.

Men may die and moulder in the dust,
Men may die and arise again from the dust,
Shoulder to shoulder in the ranks of the just,
When God is marching on.

Chorus.   Glory, &c.

WILL. Attention! make yourselves ready to march at a moments notice, (*pointing towards the Negro*) take good care of him, and you sergeant come with me (*soldiers retire to the back part of the stage.*)

(*Exeunt William and John, and soldiers.*)

SCENE IV. The garden of Miss Southworth.

MISS SOUTHWORTH, JAMES, and a SPY standing in the arbor.

SPY. Here we may talk freely; at the Mansion are too many eaves droppers.

(*Enter William, John and a soldier, making motions to one another and carefully approach the arbor.*)

JAMES. You can't trust any one of them!

MISS S. I vouch for the Major!

JAMES. And I will make the old sergeant drunk!

JOHN. (*making a fist*) Scoundrel!

SPY. Then we have nothing to fear from this picket.

MISS S. Tell your Colonel —

SPY. (*aside to Miss S.*) Shall I tell nothing except about this enterprise. He desires an answer to a letter.

MISS S. Of that, in its proper time, our own affairs must be laid aside as long as our country's cause is at stake.

SPY. He apprehends —

MISS S. Enough of that. Tell him to keep himself concealed with his men in the woods near the bridge. We will manage to keep the Major and Sergeant here, so they won't review the picket line. And if the Colonel will but capture that man below here, stationed in the hollow, then you will have no difficulty in proceeding your way under the cover of the night. You can then be in Washington day after to morrow and execute our purpose. If you go at it, you can *have the President* at a safe place before any one in Washington will miss him. Tell the Colonel to have courage and let him consider how great the achievement will be.

SPY. I will return the same way upon which I came.

(*Exit Spy.*)

JAMES. Won't I laugh to see the old sergeant make a face, who always wants to know every thing better than other people.

Miss S. Don't count chickens before they are hatched.

(During this conversation, William and John make motions to one another.) *(Exit John.)* *(Miss Southworth steps forth from the arbor, and William comes to meet her*

Will. Did you bring your business to a happy conclusion ?

Miss S. I have send an answer to my wover.

Will. Does it sound favorable ?

Miss S. For a third party, are you not curious to know — who that third party is ?

Will. No.

Miss S. *(aside)* And what does that mean ?

Will. I am only curious of something which I do not hear yet.

Miss S. What is the matter William, where are your thoughts?

Will. Only with you, my sweet Miss.

Miss S. You are so changed ! what has happened to you ?

Will. Nothing, nothing at all.

Miss S. I never saw you this way. Excuse me for a moment till your caprices — *(makes a motion to go away)*

Will. *(laying his hand on her)* Not for the world, you will stay here.

Miss S. Major. what does this mean ?

Will You don't like that do you ? but I shall soon talk to you in another voice.

Miss S. Has my kindness made you so bold ? remember you speak to a lady.

Will. I know very well I am speaking —

(A bugle sound is heard from behind the scene.)

At last !

James. Great God ! what is that ?

Will. That is for roll-call.

James. That is not the hour, neither the signal.

Will. You seem to be well versed in our signals. Well then, Miss, my men are marching to bring your Colonel over here. He might catch cold in the woods !

Traitors ! the American Union can never be destroyed by miserable plottings.

(Enter John.)

JOHN. Major the men are ready; and I dispatched an orderly to headquarters. We will have assistance, if necessary in a moment.

WILL. Won't want it; of course Miss you send your best respects to your Colonel, and now my Country and my gaurdian angel, Lenora!

(*Exit William·*) (*Music : Tramp, tramp, the Boys &c.*)

JOHN. If you want to catch us napping, you must get up earlier. (*Exit John.*)

MISS S. (*very excitedly*) What has happened ?

JAMES. They must be in league with the devil !

MISS S (*Seizing him frantically*) Have you betrayed us ?

JAMES. I hope I'll fall dead on the spot if I have.

MISS S. (*In despair*) Great God, stand by our cause, avert the terrible fate of a subjugation of our beautiful South (*jumping to her feet*) All lost — lost — lost, even he is lost, he whom I love and worship.
(*Turning to James*) Shake that empty head of yours, I love him, he is my idol. If our plan had succeeded I should have saved him, with him I was sincere. I should never have betrayed him, and now he supposes me false to him. He is deceived ! I can't survive the shock !

JAMES. Collect yourself Miss, think of saving yourself.

MISS S. Think of your own salvation, you miserable wretch ; it was only for money that you assisted me in my mighty plottings. Fly ! fly ! for such fellows as you, there is home anywhere. You don't know the two words *love* and *patriotism*, to you it is immaterial who pays you. Crawl to the feet of those Yankees and prosper.

JAMES. I can't leave you alone Miss, you will do injury to yourself.

MISS S. Oh this anguish, if it only were decided already, and that he would come and pronounce sentence over me, here on the very spot where I clasped his trembling hand and where I opened my heart to him. Only once more must I see him, tell him that I love him, then he may curse me, if he has the courage to do so !

Enter Spy.
Fly as quick as you can, we are betrayed. Dragoons are searching the country all around.

JAMES. Only assist me to save Miss Southworth.

MISS S. Away! I want no assistance

JAMES. How do matters look?

SPY. The Colonel still holds out, in a quarter of an hour they will have them all. Our plan is lost, — lost forever!

JAMES. I know a safe place at the Mansion, where we can conceal ourselves until the storm has blown over. If Miss Southworth —

MISS S. Once more! Save yourselves: I don't want your protection.

JAMES. Then come. We may yet escape.

SPY. It would be a wonder.

(Exeunt James and Spy.)
(pause.)

MISS S. It is all over, all our hope is gone, all this fair land will be under Yankee thralldom, but I will not live to see it. Let them come! these Yankees, and they shall find a corpse (*makes a motion to go, then stops. pause*)

MISS S. William! — William! —

A voice behind the scene:
"We cannot get him any further, he will die in our hands!"

(Enter John and Soldiers carrying William, who has a black handkercheif around his head.)

MISS S. (*rushing towards him*) Oh, heavens! what have I done.

JOHN. (*holding her back*) Don't disturb him, Miss; respect the sufferings of a wounded soldier. Wait, boys, let me spread my old Mantle under him (*does so*) (*Miss S. from the other side of the stage, keeps staring at William,*)
How are you now, Major?

WILL. Right well, John; is everything safe?

JOHN. Everything is right, all right. There is only a couple not caught yet. I shall stay with you, the Surgeon will be here in a minute.

WILL. I don't need him anymore.

JOHN. (*aside and sobbing*) are we that far already —

WILL. My love to my father, John.

JOHN. I will give it, sir.

WILL. Lenora, darling! I'll keep my promise: give her this letter.

JOHN. Why must I do that? There are enough others that can do it; on the long road you are now going to travel, I cannot let you go alone, I must go with you.

WILL. No, John. You must tell my father all; you must carry to him my cold body! You must tell him of my weakness, of my infidelity, of Miss Southworth, of this treason —

MISS S. (*upon the calling of her name, rushes to William*) William forgive me! forgive me!!

WILL. Miss Southworth, your dark plotting will avail you nothing. Our Union will live and will extend her blessings again over the whole Country, South as well as North

MISS S. Blessings, and I?

(Enter a Soldier.)

SOLD. Dispatch just read informing us, that Generals Sherman and Thomas have gained a great Victory at Chattanooga —

WILL. The sun rises. It is not night; it is the dawn of the Morning.

JOHN. And my William must die!

MISS S. Did ever woman suffer thus?

WILL. (*half raising himself*) Miss, you seem to be sincere in your adherence to the cause of Secession. You are erring like so many of your Country men. You cling to the sunny South; but a time will come, when you will all come to a better understanding, and you will bless us for obliging you to stay in the Union, and for extending the rule of liberty throughout the land! The day must come when all my Country men, once more, will glory in one Name, one Country, and one flag! There will be one loving family, and all animosities shall cease forever!

MISS S. He dies!

JOHN. Come nearer and see how a brave Union soldier can die! Alas!

MISS S. Only one look, one word of forgiveness!

WILL. I forgive you. He who can die for his Country, can also forgive her and his enemies: only the brave are generous. My last look for you John, my last word "*Le-nora*" (*He dies.*)

JOHN. (*after a pause*) I will get a Metallic Coffin and have it placed in a Vault and then keep it until we shall have peace. Then when we go home I will bring him to his father, so that they may rest together.

MISS S. His hand is cold, his heart beats no more.

John and the Soldiers, sing :

And when the bullet comes at last,
That pierces through the heart,
Then while his eyes are breaking,
His comrades, we are speaking,
Thus should a soldier depart.

(*Curtain Drops.*)

END OF ACT II.

———o———

ACT III.

THE NUPTIALS OR LET US HAVE PEACE.

SCENE I. A Room in the Professor's House.

PROFESSOR HUGHES, MRS. HUGHES, RICHARD NORTON, SEXTON.

PROF. Where is Lenora?

MRS. H. I do not know, I think she will be here soon.

PROF. Whenever we spend a happy hour she is sure not to be present; and when we have Company she keeps away!

RICH. Do not scold her, father. I love her as she is and when once my wife it shall be my endeavor and I shall do all to secure to her a life's happiness. The true love I bear to her will make her love me and her vivacity will return.

SCENE II. (*Enter a Grave digger. Who quietly approaches the Sexton whispering something into his ear.*)

SEXTON. No, God forbid! How could I think of doing such a thing?

PROF. What is it, Neighbor? What is the Matter?

G. DIG. (*calmly*) Something happened, Professor, were I to tell it, Mrs. Hughes might get frightened.

PROF. Speak out, for you have frightened her already.

G. DIG. Last evening, about twilight, a strange young man came to my house and ordered a grave to be dug; he said the Sexton had sent him. My wife and I were not at home at the time The grave should be near Colonel Norwood's Vault. As to day our little village is busy making preparations to receive the soldiers coming home I could not get to see the sexton about it and did the job. Now I come to inquire if he knows anything of it; but the grave is dug and the children say the strange man looked very pale. (*Pause*)

SEXTON. Well, the misfortune is not so great. Cover the grave over and as soon as somebody here in the village dies, we can use it.

G. DIG. Excuse me for having interrupted you. (*Exit*)

SEXTON. That is a very strange matter after all.

MRS. H. Indeed, it is.

PROF. Don't be foolish. Who can tell what misled or deceived the children!

MRS. H. It is a presentiment! Oh heavens! (*Raising her hands*)

PROF. Which eventually will turn out to be correct. For as we know all the people of this village it is quiet likely that before long one of our friends will die; then you will jump at the conclusion that the ordering of the grave had something to do with it. You like to think of the gloomy and mysterious. Drop that. Let us be cheerful and do not forget that we have peace and that our good brave men are coming home to day.

SCENE III. (*Enter Colonel Norwood led by a servant.*)

ALL. (*rising*) The Colonel!

COL. My dear Professor, since our unpleasantness we have

not met, I have long ago buried my anger. Aye, even at the time I felt that I was wrong, and often thought of confessing it to you. Now I thought I would stop and have a full understanding w th you. To day, you know we celebrate peace and we should all be friends.—

PROF. I was a little too hasty, Colonel—

COL. All is forgiven and forgotten — and so enough of that. The time will come when this war will be matter of impartial history. Wondering children will read of the heroic deeds of the time ; it will draw tears from the eyes of our children's children to learn what hardships their Grandfather had to endure. *We* are still in the midst of the great events and can not fully appreciate them. Now, however, we must work together, one and all, to build up again what has been destroyed and, Thank God! we can now begin to do it! All hail to the day of Appomattox !

ALL. All hail and God's blessing !

PROF. And may I ask whether your Son—

COL. God knows what the boy is doing. He has not written to me for some time. I received a letter the other day from John but I have not the patience to decipher his claw. Only so much I spelled out of it: "We are coming soon, William and I"

PROF. Well, then you may expect them every minute. How great your joy will be! To embrace your only son — as he comes crowned with honor — as one of our Country's defenders ! All the anxiety which you have felt during his absence will be forgotten in a moment !

COL. Yes, Yes! it would be all well then — if only — Professor there is something here yet, and to day it must all out. (*aside to Professor*) You have not kept your promise. —

PROF. I ? That would be the first time in my life, I failed !

MRS. H. (*aside*) Woe to us! now all is lost!

RICH. (*aside*) Thank God, he broaches the subject !

COL. At that time you solemnly promised that on the day when we would celebrate the restoration of peace and the boys would come home you would —

PROF. I would marry Lenora to our Richard. Good God! how could I forget that? But joy has overcome me so to-day. The day has not come to an end yet, though. Thank you, thank you, my worthy friend and neighbor, for this reminder; it just came in time. I understand you now. You are right, William shall not return before Lenora —

COL. That's it.

PROF. Sexton! Hurry and ask the Minister to be kind enough to perform the Marriage ceremony at church to night before he preaches his peace sermon. Please invite all our friends to the house this evening to celebrate the nuptials. They must be united this evening and you shall have my blessing, my son.

RICH. I did not want to mention the matter but since God has so willed it let us go about it with all possible dispatch.

(Exeunt Sexton and Richard.)

MRS. H. As a mother I should be grateful to you, Colonel, still it breaks my heart.

PROF. Be silent, dear Kate!

COL. Let her speak, she is the Mother.

MRS. H. Poor Lenora has not forgotten William yet and it is heartrending to observe how the poor girl worries herself about him. Since he went away, she hasn't been well for a single hour. She is pale, and disturbed, and God forgive me, sometimes I must believe that she is out of her mind! My husband don't see that for when he speaks to her she gathers all her strength to make herself appear happy. But when she is with me, alone, the portals of her grief open and sometimes I hear her weep the whole night long!

COL. My dear people! How can I help it?

PROF. My wife exaggerates. The solicitude of a mother speaks out of her.

(Enter John.)

ALL. John!

COL. Where is my son?

JOHN. (*Quietly tho hesitating*) At the Mansion.

COL. Why don't he fly into my arms?

PROF. Have you not forbidden him this house? Have not I done the same?

COL. Aye! Yes, and that commandment shall remain in force until Lenora has followed her husband over to the Springhouse. Yes, make a sour face, John, if you will, but to-day is Lenora's Wedding!

JOHN. What do I care?!

COL. What ails you? Why are you so serious and so gloomy? Speak out!

JOHN. Not here! What I have to report I shall tell you at proper quarters, in your room.

COL. You are right. Your lamentations will come early enough, but be assured of this that you'll not get me in a bad humor to night. Neither you, Mrs. Hughes, nor William with all your complaints! Professor the joy of meeting again must not be disturbed; Keep your word! I know that when he finds her a married woman all of William's passions will die away, and we shall have peace the same as the Country! Co.ae, old Grumbler!

(Exeunt Colonel and John.)

PROF Now, one word to you, my dear Kate. You must think my course in this business to be a very strange one, so let me explain to you. Sooner or later the difference of their religion would become the source of their disagreement, and to prevent her from being perhaps dishonored she must marry. Alas! Woman in our present state of Society is little better situated than she was when the ancient Greek poet wrote his Tragedy of Medea. Now keep this to yourself.

MRS. H. *(crying)* I will!

PROF. *(pressing her hand)* And now I go contended to see that all the arrangements be properly made.

(Exit Professor.)

MRS. H. *(alone)* Where can she stay? I have given my promise and I will not break it. My poor child is lost! Why should I cause her more grief? I will try to console her, but how can I do it? Perhaps I can tell her a story of his infidelity? God grant, she has not seen him already! Good Heaven, what must we suffer! The roaring of the cannon has ceased, no more news of bloody battles! Like a dove with the olive branch the news has been welcomed at every house, only in my humble cottage there is sadless grief! Would that my grey head would have been under the sod long ago, that I had never to live to see my only child broken hearted. (*Exit*)

SCENE IV.   *Open place at the gate of the Prof's. garden, as in the first act. Enter the returning volunteers (one carrying a tattered battle flag) and march over the stage. Citizens and woman rush to them and take from the soldiers their Knapsacks &c which they carry walking along side with them. The Music plays : "Johnny is marching home". Enter* LENORA *hastily running up and down the line and looking anxiously for somebody.*

ONE SOLDIER.
    Look at her!

ANOTHER SOLDIER.
    (*jestingly*) Are you going to pick one out for yourself, little girl?
    (*As the last Company is about leaving the stage Lenora in a wild shriek :*
    William! William! — all gone, and no William!
    (*Staring out in the air, she puts her hands to her head, clutching her hair which is thereby loosened and drops wildly around her shoulders*).

LENO. All have left now! Even the sun leaves me! (*it is growing darker*) Oh, how lost I feel! (*she drops down*) Oh, he is faithless! false!
    (*Enter Mrs. Hughes.*)

MRS. H. Aye! my good child, may God have Mercy upon you!

LENO. Mercy?! Mercy?! Eaven He knows no Mercy!

MRS. H. God forgive you, pray my child, a heartfelt prayer always gives consolation.

LENO. And havn't I prayed day and night? Havn't I wrung these hands till they were sore? Heaven is closed to me, my prayers don't reach there (*with a wild laugh*) I am but a poor miserable girl!

MRS. H. He may have fallen on the field of battle —

LENO. (*Leaping to her feet solemnly and with confidence*) No Mother, he has not. He swore that he would call for me even should death overtake him.

MRS. H.   Or perhaps he is not worthy of your true love and despair ; perhaps he has married some southern girl and
lives happily far away from you and perhaps is laughing
how he could deceive you! Drop him my child, think of
yourself, think of your parents !

LENO.   No! All is gone! All is lost! With God is no more
mercy ; with Man there never was! A curse! A curse
apon me, upon you all !

MRS. S.   You know not what you are saying. Your own tongue
passes Judgment upon you.   Oh, be yourself and hope
to meet him in yonder world.   Don't shut the gate of
Heaven against you, nor —

LENO.   What is Heaven? What is Hell? With him, with William is my Heaven, my Hell where he is not. With him
I fear no Hell, without him I don't want your Heaven!
You hear that?! You hear that now?! I don't want
your Heaven !

MRS. H.   Poor child! If your hopes of life are destroyed, don't
ruin yourself for eternity ; come with me and let us see
what a Mother's care and love can do.

(Exeunt Lenora leaning on the arm of Mrs. Hughes.)

SCENE V.   *Lenora's room in the Professor's House.*

Enter Mrs. H. and Lenora, from the other side the Professor and Richard

PROF.   The soldiers are coming home, the church bells are chi-
ming merrily, the bridal wreath is ready to deck your
head, in a few moments your bridegroom will lead you
to the church!

RICH.   Father, let us wait ; Lenora appears to be sick.

PROF.   I gave my word and I will keep it, *(aside to Richard)*
William is at the Mansion.   Before she hears of it she
must be your wife. *(mildly to Lenora)* I go Lenora ; your
mother will bring you the wreath. We leave you alone.
Richard will then come for you.

RICH.   *(aside to Lenora)* I obey our father, but you shall have no
cause of complaint. I shall respect your grief until time
shall make y u forget the past.   *(Exeunt Professor and
Richard.)*

(It is growing dark.

MRS. H.   *(Takes a long sad look at Lenora and as she gives no signs, Mrs.
H. exit, making gesticulations denoting great grief.   The church
bells are heard.)*

LENO. Who is being buried? Is it Lenora? — I thought she went to her wedding — Yes — in the Coffin — with whom? With her William. Won't they be merry there! I know, if the parents were not there. Yes, we now have peace. On earth there will never be peace!

(*Enter Mrs. H. with a lamp which she puts on the toilet table.*)

MRS H. Here, Lenora, your bridegroom sends you this wreath.

LENO. (*taking it*) Yes, yes! the wreath —

MRS. S Where are you Lenora?

LENO. Yes!

MRS. H. She is mad! Oh, how will this end? (*Exit Mrs. H.*)

LENO. (*Taking a position before the looking glass*) It won't become me — my hair is waving around me so wildly — I! why not — It was a fine sight anyhow when they passed by — first the Officers —

(*Noto — stands for music.*)

then the soldiers — Then I stood there all alone, (*taking the wreath and looking at it*) Why, how pretty it is, but here! Only *one* rose in it. Oh. I understand, I once heard a Song about a Rose. Those days were happy. How was that song? (*rubbing her head* Oh, my memory is all gone for I am getting old.

(*Here music sets in with the air of* "The Last Rose of Summer", *Lenora listens and at last she exclaims lively :*) That's it! That's it! That's the Song which I learned when I was young.

(*Sings.*)
> 'Tis the last rose of Summer,
> Left blooming alone ;
> All her lovely companions
> Are faded and gone :
> No flower of her kindred,
> No rosebud is nigh
> To reflect back her blushes,
> Or give sigh for sigh !

> I'll not leave thee, thou lone ones,
> To pine on the stem :
> Since the lovely are sleeping,
> Go sleep then with them :
> Thus kindly I scatter
> Thy leaves o'er the bed.
> Where thy mates of the garden
> Lie scentless and dead,

So soon may I follow,
When friendships decay ;
And from love's shining circle
Thy gems drop away !
When true hearts lie withered,
And fond ones are flown,
Oh ! who would inhabit
This bleak world alone ?

(*pause.*)

How beautiful the bride looks (*taking a seat in a chair in the back ground*) Now she is ready. She is waiting for the bridegroom !

(*Three slow knocks are heard at the garden gate, as in the first Act. At the first she is startled, at the second she eagerly listens, at the third she jumps from the chair,*)

Oh, Heavens ! 'Tis William ! Yes (*wildly*) it is he ! He promised to come for me — at the grave yard ! His horse is standing saddled ! (*opens the window, the pale vision of William is seen outside*) Oh, William ! And is it you ?! How pale and gloomy your face looks !? You come to take me away with you. William, I am ready ! Your true love is ready to follow ! Oh, I cried so much about you ! William, they say, you were either false or dead, but you live and you keep your promise, so do I, William ! Already I have the wreath upon my head ; the candles are lit on the Altar ! They want to drag me to church ! but you are my bridegroom. Oh ! Oh ! (*shivering*) how cold it is, how coldly the wind blows — (*going away from the window*) Hear the jingling of his spurs! — Howl wind — Farewell Mother ! I fly into William's arms — on William's wild horse — and then away ! Away ! In flying canter — Away ! Farther and farther through the cold night, then vanish the houses — the meadows — the rivulets — the country — before our eyes — then the bridges thunder under his horse's hoof — Away, with him to the wedding — I come William ! — I come —   (*Exit Lenora.*)

SCENE VI. *Enter Mrs. Hughes, Professor, Richard and Sexton*

Mrs. H. Lenora ? Where is the child ?

Prof. (*coming in right after her*) Are you ready, my daughter ?

Mrs. H. I don't see her. I hope she did not —

(*Enter Richard.*)

RICH. *interrupting Mrs. H.*) The solemn hour has arrived.

PROF. We miss Lenora !

(*Enter the Sexton hurriedly through the middle door.*)

SEXTON They are waiting for you at the church.

ALL. Where is Lenora ?

SEXTON. I don't know whether I may venture to tell —

MRS. H. For God's sake speak !

SEXTON. I was standing in the entryway waiting for you to come, then she rushed by me as pale as death, her eyes glowing, I thought she had lost her reason.

MRS. H. Yes ! Yes ! proceed !

SEXTON. I wanted to stop her, but she tore loose from me, and cried bitterly : "Farewell old man ! I go to my wedding." Well, says I, Miss Lenora but not withont a bridegroom, and he is inside with your father. "You lie !" says she, "He is waiting for me with his horse at the graveyard. William is there. My love to father and mother. I shall never come back !" Thus she rushed out of the door, and outside the wind was blowing, rain falling ! The weather is terrible !

PROF. *(excitedly)* Woman, you turn pale ! You know of it speak ! What has occurred ?

MRS. H. *(In great anxiety)* Could it be possible ? She told me a hundred times that William would elope with her upon his return from the war. It cannot be !

PROF. Shall this disgrace undo me ?

RICH. Such an outrage would be uuheard of—

PROF. *Grasping his hand)* Come ! come to the Mansion. To him, to his father ! I shall call for an account and for satisfaction from him ! The old —

MRS. H. Oh ! don't blame me for it.

PROF. Follow me ! If our honor is dear to you. It is yet time that we may save them.

(*Exeunt all.*)

SCENE VII. *A graveyard, in the back ground a church lit up. On the side is a family vault with iron gates. out of which a dim light is appearing, next to the vault is a newly made grave.*

Enter William's Ghost followed by Lenora staggering slowly towards the edge of the grave.

LENO   At last! At last! Oh, William, that was a long, long,
        road! Now get off! Alight from your horse; here is
        the place, here is our little home, very narrow, but get
        in.   *Ghost vanishes*) It is so cold (*shivering*) Good night!
        Good night! (*she sinks beside the grave and dies. Music is heard
        from the church, during which enter Colonel, John and Attendants
        coming from the Vault and carrying lanterns.*)

COL.   Thank God, that's done! The Coffin is safely deposited
        in our Vault, and soon mine will stand beside it. I will
        not weep.   John, did he not die for his Country?

JOHN.   Cheerfuly, and like a hero!

COL.   Peace be to his ashes! What goes on in the church?

ONE OF THE ATTENDANTS:

        Why? Colonel, it is Miss Lenora's wedding:

JOHN.   (*aside*) I have not yet delivered his letter to her.

COL.   Lenora's wedding? Now there need not have been so
        much hurry about it. My poor William would not have
        disturbed them.

PROF.   (*Behind the scene*) There he is!
        (*Enter Professor, Richard, Mrs. Hughes and Sexton.*)

PROF.   Colonel!—Man! Where is your son?

COL.   In the Vault!

ALL.   Ah!

PROF.   Where is Lenora?

JOHN.   (*now seeing Lenora's corpse*) Here on the grave, and *Death*
        was her bridegroom!

ALL.   Lenora! (*group around her*)

JOHN.   He has come for her! He has kept his promise and I
        will keep mine! Here is his letter, poor girl! (*laying
        William's letter upon her body.*)

ONE OF THE ATTENDANTS:

        Now we know who ordered that grave.

PROF.   She is dead!

JOHN.   (*with bitterness*) Now close that iron gate of the Vault, so
        they cannot come together

COL.   They are united.

MRS. H. Oh God! my child! my child!

        (*Enter Miss Southworth in deep mourning and walks slowly towards
        the Colonel.*)

JOHN. *(aside to the Colonel)* That is the one!

MISS S. Colonel Norwood? *(the Colonel nods)* Oh, Colonel, have mercy on a poor distressed woman who is wretched. I, Colonel, come to accuse myself of having caused the death of your son, your William, whom I worshiped, I thought at the time I was doing right, but I see now that I was sadly erring. I mistook treason for patriotsm. Oh, sir, I have had no peace since that dreadful occurance. During the days I pray that night may come, and during the night I pray that day may break; but the night does not afford me the relief of a sweet slumber and the day has nothing to divert my mind from the terrible recollection. Oh, sir! there is but one hope left whereby to appease my guilty conscience. Oh, sir! *(kneeling before him)* say but two words: "I forgive"

COL. Madam, arise! I wish not to see an American humbled. You were an erring sister; but you are a sister still! Your error has been atoned for! Let it be forgotten, and only the sister remembered Although, it has cost me my only son my only child! Still I have malice towards none, but charity for all. From the bottom of my heart I forgive you. "LET US HAVE PEACE."

(Pause)

PROF. Glory to God in the highest, and on earth peace, good will towards men

JOHN. *(coming to the front of the stage.)*

(Sings.)   Were I but in that dark cold grave,
I then should be at ease, —

pause.

(In a crying voice But since our William has left me,
Death of my friends bereft me,
Old John shall find no peace!

(Curtain Drops.)

END OF ACT III.

——— o ———

NOTE—The songs on Pages 7, 22, 23 and 34 are taken from "THE GRAND ARMY OF THE REPUBLIC SONGSTER," and are inserted in this play with the kind permission of the Publisher ROBERT M. DEWITT Esq., No. 33 Rose Street, New York.

www.ingramcontent.com/pod-product-compliance
Lightning Source LLC
Chambersburg PA
CBHW030722110426
42739CB00030B/1276